WORDS *of* HOPE *and* HEALING

NATURE HEALS

Reconciling Your Grief
Through Engaging
with the Natural World

Alan D. Wolfelt, Ph.D.

Companion
PRESS

An imprint of the Center for Loss and Life Transition | Fort Collins, Colorado

Companion Press is an imprint of the Center for Loss and Life Transition,
3735 Broken Bow Road, Fort Collins, Colorado 80526.

26   25   24   23   22   21   6   5   4   3   2   1

ISBN: 978-1-61722-301-3

CONTENTS

Welcome 1

The Nature of Grief and Mourning 5

Nature Deprivation and You 9

The Science of Nature as Healer 13

    Physical health 13

    Cognitive health 15

    Take a forest bath 16

    Emotional health 17

    Social health 18

    Spiritual health 19

    How many minutes? 20

Nature as Grief Therapist 21

How to Use Nature Therapy in Grief 27

Integrating Mourning Into Nature 29

Getting Out Into Nature 33

    Your immediate environment 33

Your neighborhood and community 35

The art of sitting still 37

Farther afield 38

Using ceremony in nature 40

Bringing Nature In 43

Plants. 44

Natural materials 44

Nature imagery 45

Animals 46

Natural food. 47

Aromatherapy 47

Nature sounds 48

A Final Word 49

The Natural Griever's Bill of Rights 51

WELCOME

"The best remedy for those who are afraid, lonely, or unhappy is to go outside…I firmly believe that nature brings solace in all troubles."
— Anne Frank

If you've picked up this book, you are no doubt hurting.

The pain is difficult to bear, I know, but it's also normal. When we experience a great loss of any kind—death, divorce, serious illness or injury, job loss, or any other unwanted, significant change—we naturally suffer. We feel deep, ongoing pain.

I've been a grief counselor and educator for more than forty years. During this span, I've been privileged to bear witness to the grief of thousands of people. I've been a humble companion to them on their journeys. They've taught me that their pain is a natural and even necessary part of love.

Your pain, too, is natural and necessary. But even when we acknowledge its necessity, it still hurts. It's still grueling and agonizing.

Understandably, you seek relief from your pain. In an attempt to make the hurt more tolerable or even disappear for a while, people usually first turn to the coping mechanisms they're most accustomed to. You might distract yourself with technology and entertainment. You may numb yourself with alcohol or drugs. You might travel, hoping you can leave your pain behind you. You might try to keep yourself busy.

With the exception of alcohol and drug overuse, all of these coping strategies are fine and effective to some degree. It's OK to include them in your grief survival toolkit. But what we're here to consider today is that there are more beneficial ways of integrating and softening the natural pain of your grief. In this book we'll focus on one in particular—one you may haven't relied on to any great extent before.

Of course, I'm talking about nature. Nature heals. Not only can engaging with the natural world ease your pain right now—today and tomorrow—it can supercharge your longer-term journey to healing. I've seen it firsthand, up close, over and over again.

About thirty-five years ago, when I was designing the campus of the Center for Loss and Life Transition, it was of the utmost importance to me that nature take centerstage. Perched on the foothills of the Rocky Mountains in northern

Colorado, the Center enjoys views of the city of Fort Collins to the east and higher mountain foothills to the west. Evergreens and stunning rock formations surround the building. To take advantage of this spectacular but rugged setting, we added extensive decking, boardwalks from one area to another, gazebos with seating, and a number of benches.

Weather permitting, grief counseling sessions often take place in these sacred outdoor spaces. The grounds of the Center for Loss are a sanctuary for mourners—a place they can get away from the demands of their daily lives and give dedicated attention to their grief and mourning. Some people who have a hard time talking about their loss in the indoor spaces of the Center instantly relax and open up the moment we do a little walking outdoors and sit down together in the gazebo. I believe I'm a compassionate grief companion, but nature is the true healer.

Nature can help heal you, too. If you're not a "nature person," that's not a problem. You'll find that a little nature goes a long way. You don't have to become a nature fanatic to avail yourself of the healing power of nature. Even if you live in a crowded city, even if you have a busy life that keeps you indoors most of the time, even if you don't particularly enjoy nature or think of yourself as the outdoorsy type, there are ways to integrate small doses of nature into your everyday life that can have outsized, positive effects on your life and healing.

That's because nature and grief naturally go together. Thank you for entrusting me to show you how and to help you discover ways to use nature to cope with and heal your grief.

THE NATURE OF GRIEF
AND MOURNING

"Nature is our greatest teacher, of surrender, of allowing, of simply being. Every blade of grass, every flower, every tree remembers. This moment. This present. This is where life is."

— Alexandra Domelle

Let's start by defining grief. Grief is a natural internal experience that follows a separation from anyone or anything we are strongly attached to.

If we are lucky, we love. When we experience separation and loss, our love shows up as grief.

Grief is everything we think and feel inside ourselves about the separation and loss. Grief typically includes lots of different emotions, including shock, disbelief, confusion, yearning, anxiety, anger, guilt, sadness, numbness, and many more.

Grief also includes all of our thoughts about the loss. Our minds wonder about what happened. They try to make sense of it by building connections, replaying memories, and imagining scenarios. And our minds also wonder about what will happen in the future. We naturally think through our story of love and loss.

Love is natural. Grief is natural. Like the natural world around us, they are both wild, unpredictable, uncontrollable, awe-inspiring things.

Also natural is mourning. Mourning is the outward expression of our internal grief. Crying is a form of mourning, and when we are grieving, our bodies naturally cry to release stress chemicals and to signal to those around us that we are in pain. Telling others about our loss is another way of mourning. It's natural to want to talk about what happened, share memories, and wonder our grief thoughts aloud.

Mourning, too, is wild, unpredictable, uncontrollable, and awe-inspiring. It's also healing. Over time and through ongoing expression, grief befriended and communicated is grief healed.

Some years ago I pinpointed the natural mourning needs we all have in common. While our grief and mourning journeys are unique in their particulars, we share the following six mourning needs, regardless of the type and particular circumstances of the loss we are suffering.

THE SIX NEEDS OF MOURNING

Need 1: Acknowledge the reality of the loss

Need 2: Embrace the pain of the loss

Need 3: Remember the moments and circumstances that formed the attachment and deepened it over time

Need 4: Develop a new self-identity

Need 5: Search for meaning

Need 6: Reach out for and accept support from others

Mourning is active expression of our grief, and when we engage day-to-day with one or more of the six needs of mourning, we are taking a small step toward healing.

Now imagine engaging with nature and intentional mourning combined. Talk about a dynamic duo. We'll discuss this further on page 29.

NATURE DEPRIVATION AND YOU

"If there is one thing clear about the centuries dominated by the factory and the wheel, it is that although the machine can make everything from a spoon to a landing-craft, a natural joy in earthly living is something it never has and never will be able to manufacture."

— Henry Beston

Are you nature-deprived much of the time? Many of us are.

It wasn't always that way. Throughout human history, people lived mostly in rural settings and had a strong, symbiotic relationship with nature. They hunted, fished, gathered, and, later, farmed.

The industrial revolution that began in the early 1800s increasingly brought us indoors. We started to work in factories, and we centralized food production. Soon electricity brought lights as bright as sunlight into our homes and workplaces. Furnaces, air conditioning, and readily available upholstered furniture made the indoors more comfortable. Cities grew, while rural areas lost population.

In recent decades, the rise of computer technology has hastened this shift. We now interact more with computers than we do with anything else in our environment or with other people. According to Nielsen, we're now spending on average more than ten hours a day on computers, phones, TVs, and game consoles.

We're sitting more and moving less. And we're doing it inside. According to the EPA, the average American spends ninety-three percent of their time indoors.

Many scientists now believe that human beings are genetically and evolutionarily programmed to connect with nature. We were one with nature for 2.2 million years, and our recent shift away from our symbiosis with nature has been relatively abrupt. We're living in a time of transition, and if we are to disconnect from nature (which I certainly hope we're not!), it will take many more generations for us to fully adapt.

In his bestselling 2005 book *Last Child in the Woods*, author Richard Louv coined the term "nature deficit disorder" to describe the consequences of humanity's modern-day alienation from nature. He believes that a lack of connection with nature has caused widespread anxiety, depression, and attention disorders. I know that I'm more relaxed and in a better mood when I've spent time outdoors. I'm also better able to focus.

These same symptoms—anxiety, depression, and an inability to concentrate—are also common in grief. If you're grieving *and* you're nature-deprived, then, are some of your grief symptoms exacerbated unnecessarily? I think they often are.

THE SCIENCE OF
NATURE AS HEALER

*"Study nature, love nature, stay close to nature.
It will never fail you."*
— Frank Lloyd Wright

In recent decades, as we have become increasingly disconnected from nature, scientists have been studying how our bodies and minds respond when we return to nature. Their findings can help us better understand the many ways in which we can use nature to help us cope with our grief in the short-term and heal our grief in the longer-term. You might be surprised at the powerful, myriad benefits nature offers us.

PHYSICAL HEALTH

A couple of years ago, doctors in Scotland began writing "nature prescriptions" for their patients with chronic illnesses. They created a calendar with activity suggestions such as combing beaches for shells, gardening, and searching for otters during low tide. The experiment was so successful that the concept has since been rolled out in other countries.

Spending time in nature has been shown to have numerous physical benefits. It lowers blood pressure and heart rate. Crucially, it also lowers levels of the stress chemical cortisol in your body. When you're in danger, cortisol rushes more glucose to your bloodstream, suppresses the digestive system, and puts you on alert so you're prepared to flee or fight. That's helpful in emergencies, but when cortisol levels remain high over time due to chronic stress, you're at risk for a whole host of problems ranging from anxiety to heart disease, weight gain, and sleep problems.

Speaking of sleep, nature time improves sleep quality because exposure to sunlight during the daytime helps regulate your sleep cycle. What's more, fifteen to twenty minutes of sunshine each day helps your body better absorb vitamin D, which strengthens your bones and reduces your risk for certain diseases, including cancer.

And then there's the immune-system boost you get from getting outdoors. Did you know that many plants release organic compounds called phytoncides? These airborne chemicals have natural antibacterial and antifungal qualities. Miraculously, when you breathe them in, your body gets better at fighting viruses and even tumors. Wow!

Researchers have determined that all of these physical benefits of spending time in nature are independent of exercise. In other words, you don't have to be moving around outside to reap the rewards; simply sitting or resting in a natural setting activates these positive changes. BUT! But when you add exercise, the physical rewards of nature time are even greater. Your blood flow improves, bringing more oxygen to all the cells of your body and further lowering blood pressure and heart rate. Your muscles get stronger and your joints more flexible. And physical activity also releases happy brain chemicals called endorphins. Sprinkle endorphins on top of all the rest and you're more likely to feel happiness. In short, outdoor exercise amplifies all of the other physical health benefits we've discussed so far as well as the cognitive, emotional, social, and spiritual benefits we'll be reviewing next.

COGNITIVE HEALTH

If you're not thinking clearly, go for a short nature walk.

People who take a walk in a natural setting perform twenty percent better on cognitive tests than those who take a stroll in a city or indoors. Why? Because in an urban setting, or when interacting with technology, our minds are forced to think about possible dangers and problem solving. Basically, encounters with other people, with buildings and other manmade environments, with advertising and media, as well as the constant decision-making required of navigating these situations, are cognitively fatiguing.

When we're in nature, on the other hand, our minds are free. Our brains can let their guards down and relax. Gazing at a sunset or an ocean view are other good examples of this phenomenon. I'm sure you know what this feels like. Most of us enjoy these activities because they're both beautiful and nontaxing. They don't require anything of our brains or bodies but to be present and enjoy.

We're also less likely to ruminate when we're in nature, according to scientists. That is, we're less prone to focusing repetitively on problems or worries. In natural environments, our thoughts are more apt to drift freely and peacefully.

Nature time gives our brains a break. Most of us can't spend a majority of our lives in nature, but we can intentionally build short nature interludes into our days. These cognitive respites courtesy of nature prepare us to return refreshed to our more challenging activities and environments. Our brains are rested, our short-term memories sharpened, and our ability to focus restored.

TAKE A FOREST BATH

The Japanese practice of *shinrin-yoku*, or forest bathing, has become popular the world over. Studies have shown that forest bathing has all of the positive effects we've been discussing in this section on cognitive health.

Nature Heals

To forest bathe, you simply enter a natural space and engage with it using all five of your senses. Walk in the forest if you are able. Or try sitting on a log or lying down in a meadow.

Activate all your senses. Run your hand down the trunk of a tree. Listen to the birds and the breeze. Smell the fragrance of the leaves, plant materials, dirt, and fungi. Breathe deeply, and exhale slowly.

There is no right or wrong to forest bathing, but do leave your technology at home. Savor the beauty and the sensory feast. Stay as long as it takes for you to feel relaxed and re-centered.

Once you have some experience with forest bathing, you'll find you can do it any natural setting in any weather. You are present to nature, as nature is always present to you.

EMOTIONAL HEALTH

The green of nature is emotional gold.

One study of a million people persuasively arrived at the conclusion that children raised in neighborhoods with the least amount of green space or easy access to nature—independent of affluence and other variables—were fifty-five percent more likely to be mentally unwell.

It makes sense. When our bodies feel better and our minds are relaxed, our emotions tend to follow. Spending time in nature has been proven to improve our mood, reduce feelings of anger, increase resilience, and even boost self-esteem. It eases depression and anxiety. It's simply an all-around emotional tonic.

Something important to keep in mind is that nature offers these emotional benefits regardless of setting or season. Studies show that engaging with any natural environment in any weather improves emotional wellbeing. Even if you prefer a certain landscape—the beach, perhaps, or the mountains— or a certain season of the year, please remember that spending time in whatever natural environments are most convenient to you, year-round, will be essential to your self-care.

SOCIAL HEALTH

Activities that improve our physical, cognitive, and emotional wellbeing tend to improve our social health as well. That's because when our bodies and minds are well and our mood is good, we're much more likely to interact with others in positive, meaningful ways.

The science supports this. Australian researchers found that people who spend time in a green space at least once a week are more comfortable in social situations. Children who are allowed to play freely in natural spaces are better able to connect socially during their play. And especially for people who live alone or in relative isolation, getting outside the four walls of their homes gives them a chance to interact with others in natural settings.

Green spaces in neighborhoods and communities provide places for people to interact in healthy ways. Parks and playgrounds are gathering spaces that build a sense of familiarity and community. Nature is a simple bonder. But even when nature fosters healthy solitude, it returns people to their social settings better prepared to be with others.

SPIRITUAL HEALTH

Natural settings are spiritual settings. We tend to feel a connection with the divine when we are on a mountaintop or when we look up at a night sky full of stars. We feel awe. We sense that we are part of something much larger, and our own troubles, no matter how painful, seem less significant in the grand scheme of things.

What's more, nature surprises and inspires us. The more present we are in nature, the more we notice. And the more we notice, the more awed we become at the miraculous sky, plants, trees, rocks and sand, water features, and animals. From the majestic to the miniscule—and everything in between—we find wonder upon wonder.

Studies show that spending time in nature induces brain waves similar to those generated during meditation. Nature feels sacred and mysterious. And that connection to the sacred helps us get in touch with our divine sparks—that still, small voice inside us that whispers of life's meaning and purpose.

Our spirits and souls are powerfully drawn to nature. In nature we more readily contemplate our beliefs and values. We are better able to transcend the mundane realities of our lives and consider the boundlessness and timelessness of the universe. We crave nature in large part because we crave these special moments of epiphany and transcendence.

HOW MANY MINUTES?

How much time do you have to spend engaging with nature to feel positive effects?

Recently, one large study in England determined that a total of 120 minutes a week spent in nature was sufficient for people to report high levels of wellbeing. The research showed that those two hours could be split up among many brief outings, several half-hour sessions, or a single exposure. The study also controlled for physical activity, so the 120-minute threshold applied whether people were exercising or sitting on a park bench.

I definitely don't think you need to follow a regimented nature schedule. Grief and healing are esoteric matters that defy measurement. But it might help you to know that engaging with nature for just seventeen minutes a day, on average, is likely to have a big impact on your life.

NATURE AS GRIEF THERAPIST

"You didn't come into this world. You came out of it,
like a wave from the ocean. You are not a stranger here."
— Alan Watts

Now that we've reviewed all the many ways that spending time in nature can benefit us physically, cognitively, emotionally, socially, and spiritually throughout our lives, let's talk about how nature helps us during times of grief in particular.

First of all, nature time softens many if not all of the normal symptoms of grief. Because it eases anxiety, depression, anger, stress, and more, it tempers the "bad" feelings. And because it boosts endorphins, self-esteem, resilience, joy, and more, it heightens the "good" feelings. Nature helps balance us out.

Now, the truth is that are really no bad or good feelings in grief. All feelings are normal and equally valid—the dark and the light emotions—and it's necessary to befriend and express any and all emotions you may be experiencing as part of your grief. But as we noted in this book's introduction, we do need relief from our more difficult feelings sometimes, and engaging with nature provides this relief.

You might think of nature as a shock absorber for your grief. Entering a natural space and joining with the calm can feel a bit like wrapping a soft cushion around yourself. Your grief is still there; it goes wherever you go. But all of the extra stress and tension that are not truly part of the essence of your grief fall away. You feel safer there, and this allows you to become a more active participant in your grief.

That extra stress and tension come from concurrent stressors in our lives—our jobs, our financial obligations, our family responsibilities, etc.— but they also come from "dirty pain." Clean pain is the normal pain we feel after difficult life experiences. Dirty pain is the damaging, multiplied pain we create when we catastrophize, judge ourselves, or allow ourselves to be judged by others. Dirty pain is the bleak "what-if" stories we conjure up in our minds and the imaginary obstacles we put in our own way. It's human nature to fall prey to dirty pain, but it' not strictly necessary. And when we enter a natural landscape, the dirty pain tends to drop away, leaving only the pure, clean pain for us to confront.

Second, because nature has a calming effect, and because it naturally softens even our clean pain, it can make it a little easier for us to engage with that pain in doses. Basically, spending time in nature can make the pain feel more manageable for a short time, and while it's more manageable, we may be able to embrace it more readily.

The calm of nature also allows for the transition from "soul work" to "spirit work." According to psychologist Carl Jung, soul work is the downward movement of the psyche. It is the willingness to connect with what is dark, deep, and not necessarily pleasant. Spirit work, on the other hand, involves the upward, ascending movement of the psyche. It is during spirit work that you find renewed meaning and joy in life. But soul work comes before spirit work. It lays the ground for spirit work. The spirit cannot ascend until the soul first descends, and nature provides a safe, calming environment in which the soul can naturally descend.

This means that we can effectively use nature time for intentional mourning and for intentional encounters with the six needs of mourning. This is a powerful combination, and we'll be talking more about it under the subtitle "Integrating Mourner Into Nature," on page 29.

Essentially, nature offers our grief hospitality. As the theologian Henri Nowen famously said, "Hospitality is the creation of free space where the stranger can enter and become a friend. Hospitality is not to change people but to offer them space where change can take place." Nature offers us that safe space where we can befriend our grief and change can begin to take place.

Third, nature implicitly teaches us about the natural cycles of life and death. When we regularly spend time outdoors, we see the seasons change. We are witness to the migrations of animals. We watch plants grow, die, and grow again. These never-ending cycles remind us that change, destruction, and rebirth are fundamental to life on earth. Yet at the same time, the constancy of nature promises that no matter what happens, it is always there for us.

Fourth, nature is a kind of companion. Have you noticed that when you enter nature you may be by yourself but you tend not to feel alone? I call my philosophy of grief counseling "companioning" because I believe in being present to and bearing witness to mourners. I'm not there to treat them, tell them what to do, or be the expert. They are the expert of their grief. Instead, I'm there to walk beside them, help them feel safe, and give them an arm to hold onto now and then. Nature acts in much the same way. It is always there for you, steady and calming.

And finally, nature is a neutral, nonjudgmental backdrop

against which we can be who and what we are. Nature is natural, and in nature, we can be our natural selves. We don't have to pretend. We don't have to conform to social expectations. We don't have to look or act a certain way. Instead, we can feel what we feel and think what we think and behave as we wish.

Spiritual guru Ram Dass suggested that we should accept each other and ourselves in the same way that we accept trees:

> *"When you go out into the woods, and you look at the trees, you see all these different trees. And some of them are bent, and some of them are straight, and some of them are evergreens, and some of them are whatever. And you look at the tree and you allow it. You see why it is the way it is. You sort of understand that it didn't get enough light, and so it turned that way. You appreciate the tree.*
>
> *"The minute you get near humans, you lose all that. And you are constantly saying, 'You are too this, or I'm too this.' That judgment mind comes in. And so I practice turning people into trees. Which means appreciating them just as they are."*

As you journey through grief, I hope will you remember to turn yourself into a tree. You are wonderful and worthy just as you are. You are a singular part of nature, just like a unique tree. I think spending time among trees as you grieve will help reinforce this crucial message.

HOW TO USE NATURE
THERAPY IN GRIEF

"Everything in nature invites us constantly to be what we are."
— Gretel Ehrlich

Before we talk through some specific ways in which you can engage with nature—outdoors and indoors—let's cover some fundamental guidelines.

First, there are no guidelines. Ha! Spending regular time in nature will help you heal, period. So do whatever works for you.

I encourage you to explore and to find activities and places you enjoy. I'd wager that there are a number of parks, trails, and natural spaces located within a few minutes of your home that you didn't even realize were there. Make it a mission to find and get to know all of them. And while you're at it, try some new outdoor activities, as well. Nature will help open your mind and your heart, and you just might find yourself open to outdoor experiences you weren't interested in before.

You might also find it meaningful to explore outdoor activities and places associated with the person who died or with your loss. If there's a special park or bike ride or fishing hole that helps you connect with your grief, that's probably a good spot to visit now and then.

If you're busy or an "indoorsy" type, I would also encourage you to preschedule nature time into your day. For some, it's easy for weeks to slip past with little or no daily engagement with nature. To prevent this from happening, you'll probably need to be very intentional about spending a couple of hours a week outside if you can. Remember that magic 120 minutes we talked about on page 20? That might be the only real guideline I hope you'll follow.

When you enter nature, go alone or with others. You don't have to venture into the wilderness by yourself to have a transformational experience. No—the whole point here is to find ways to regularly dose yourself with short encounters with nature, sometimes alone and sometimes in the company of friends or family. Both can be effective parts of your nature therapy.

INTEGRATING MOURNING INTO NATURE

"I go to nature to be soothed, healed,
and have my senses put in order."
— John Burroughs

Simply allowing yourself to feel your grief when you're in nature will help you heal. Because nature time provides so many benefits, you don't have to do anything special while you're there to feel more calm, centered, and even happy. You can absolutely think of some of your nature time as necessary respite from your grief.

But if you add active mourning to your nature time now and then, you will supercharge your healing. As we've said, mourning is the outward expression of your inner grief. It gives divine momentum to your grief. Actively mourning in nature is essentially a double dose of healing—or even a quadruple dose, for this is one of those things where the whole is greater than the sum of its parts.

So how do you mourn in nature? As with all things in grief,

there is no right way or wrong way—there is only what works for you. I'll give you some suggestions here to get you thinking, and you can use them as springboards to come up with your own ideas and plans.

One fundamental is to welcome your tears of grief while you're in nature. If you feel like crying, sobbing, or wailing, allow yourself to openly do so. You have been wounded, and just as all natural beings express their wounds in some way, you may do so by crying. If you're in an isolated area, you can sob as loudly as you want to. If not, it's still OK to cry quietly. Remember that sadness is just as valid an emotion as any other, and expressing it is an essential part of being human.

Likewise, if anger is part of your grief journey, you can express it in nature through actions such as screaming, throwing stones, or stomping your way through the underbrush. Try sitting at the edge of a body of water and tossing rocks into the water. The physical action of moving your arm and body will dissipate some of your bodily tension, and the repetition of the motion, the sights, and the sounds will naturally soothe your anger.

Gathering natural items like sticks, pinecones, or stones on your outdoor forays is another outdoor mourning activity. Take these objects home with you and use them to create art that helps express your grief.

Now that you're getting the idea of actively mourning in nature, let's think back to the six needs of mourning (page 7). Intentionally working on them while you're in nature is an excellent way to combine nature time with mourning.

For example, the third mourning need is to remember the moments and circumstances that formed the attachment and deepened it over time. In other words, Need 3 is memory work. If you bring photos or albums with you into nature and spend time there carefully looking them over and embracing the memories they conjure, you're engaging with Need 3. (And I know I told you to leave your phone at home, but if you'll be using your phone to look through photos, I'll allow it.☺) Sitting at a table in your back yard or on a patio while you assemble a memory box or photo album is another way to do this. A third way would be to write memories in a journal or a letter while you're in nature. And a fourth way would be to sit or walk outdoors with a friend while you tell them about your memories.

I hope you'll find ways to use nature time for solace and respite as well as for actively mourning. The former will provide you with the doses of rejuvenation you need during grief, and the latter will accelerate your momentum toward healing.

GETTING OUT INTO NATURE

"Come forth into the light of things. Let nature be your teacher."
— William Wordsworth

There are lots of ways to get out into nature, and they all count. You don't have to hike to a cabin in the woods, climb Mount Everest, or sail to a remote island to consider yourself immersed in nature. A tiny courtyard with a tree and a few plants may be enough. So think simple, small, and nearby to start with, then go from there.

YOUR IMMEDIATE ENVIRONMENT

Step out your front door or onto your patio. Where are you? Are you within a few steps of shrubs, trees, plants, rocks, gardens, and grass or natural ground cover? Do you have a view to the sky? If so, you're already in nature. Regularly accessing the natural world right outside your home is the easiest way to add more nature time to your life.

I've noticed that some people don't tend to hang out in the outdoor spaces adjacent to their homes because they don't have a good spot to sit. If this applies to you, I'd encourage you to invest in a comfortable chair. Of course, it can be a lightweight folding chair if you need to carry it in and out. If it feels awkward sitting in the outdoor locations available to you, try bringing a book with you.

Another reason that many people today don't avail themselves of the nature right outside their homes is they have a hard time disconnecting from technology. If you're addicted to technology—and if you are, don't be ashamed; it's built into our world right now—I encourage you to make a pact with yourself to walk away from your phone, computer, tablet, and TV for five-minute intervals at least once each hour. You can set a reminder on your phone if you'd like. During those short breaks, simply stand and head outside. Spend a few minutes walking, gardening, meditating, or simply sitting and gazing.

If, on the other hand, the spaces outside your home have little flora and fauna and/or aren't conducive to sitting and relaxing, you may have to go farther afield for your daily nature fixes. The closest green space or park will work. Walk there and back if you're able for an extra health boost. I would be remiss if I didn't affirm that the outdoors is not equally accessible to everyone, however. While most cities have parks and open spaces, these green oases are not always

Nature Heals

sufficiently large, numerous, or well-distributed. Still, there is usually enough nature nearby for it to offer more of a benefit than you may realize.

And as you become more engaged with nature and feel its healing power in your life, you might even want to consider relocating to a living situation with better access to nature. Who knows—you may even be able to find a less-expensive home or apartment surrounded by lusher nature—a compelling and wise tradeoff.

Finally, if you have limited mobility, I understand that you may need accommodations or assistance getting out into nature. Yet you deserve nature time just as much as anyone else does, so I hope you will be proactive in advocating for yourself and seek assistance when you need it. The ideas under Bringing Nature In, page 43, may also be of particular interest to you.

YOUR NEIGHBORHOOD AND COMMUNITY

Walking or biking in your neighborhood and community is a wonderful way to get outside and also build relationships with neighbors, shopkeepers, etc. Get to know the parks, gardens, and nature preserves near your home. And don't forget cemeteries! They are often beautiful, quiet outdoor spaces perfect for contemplation of life and death while you stroll or sit on a bench.

Find different spots to go in different weather—somewhere shaded when it's sunny, somewhere sheltered when it's rainy or windy, somewhere open when you want to feel the sun on your face.

Explore various ways of being in these natural spaces. Pack a picnic and invite a friend. Bring a book and read. Bird watch. Join a tai chi group or hiking club. Volunteer to help maintain a community garden. Play tennis or pickleball. Identify tree species in your town. Watch the sun rise. As I've mentioned, exercising in nature is a good staple because it multiplies benefits. If you've been exercising indoors, try doing the same thing outdoors instead. Why walk on a treadmill when you can walk on a lakeshore path? And if there's a labyrinth for meditative walking in your community, I urge you to give it a try.

Choose activities that feel engaging to you, but don't feel that you need to take on extra effort or commitments if you're not ready. As studies have shown, simply sitting in nature can be lifechanging.

THE ART OF SITTING STILL

Grief asks you to withdraw before you are ready to emerge into the busyness of life again. You have probably felt like being alone at times since the loss. You may have parked yourself on the couch for days at a time. You might have shut yourself up in your bedroom and crawled under the covers.

This instinct to self-isolate is often strong, especially early in grief. The numbness of early grief settles in like fog. We instinctively withdraw and shut down. This is normal, but if you are still in that early withdrawal phase, I would encourage you to spend some of your isolation time in nature.

"Nature can bring you to stillness. That is its gift to you."
— Eckhart Tolle

Today, it's easy to self-isolate with technology. Even if people are all around you, you can lose yourself in your phone or TV. The trouble is, this form of self-isolation, while entertaining and a good occasional break from reality, does not soothe your soul.

The next time you feel like being alone, try ditching your devices and instead heading out into nature. Find a place to be still. Silence is also important and sacred. The relative quiet of nature helps the manmade demands of the "real world" to fall away. Have you noticed that most nature sounds are fine, though? I believe it's because the most primitive part of our brains, which keeps us alert to danger, perceives sounds like birdsong, rustling leaves, and lapping waves as safe. When we are observing nature with our eyes and listening to it with our ears, we feel one with its harmony.

So go to your quiet place in nature and simply sit, relax your muscles, and breathe deeply. Close your eyes if you want to, or maintain a soft focus. If thoughts are bothering you, calm your mind by drawing attention to your breath. Allow yourself to feel the air on your skin and smell the aromas wafting by. Sit still in this manner for at least ten minutes—preferably longer.

Solitude, stillness, and silence in nature are natural fits. In practicing the art of sitting still out-of-doors, you will find yourself.

FARTHER AFIELD

If you're drawn to a certain type of natural environment that doesn't exist in your community, by all means, travel to nature if and when you can. This doesn't replace the need to interact with close-to-home nature on a daily basis, but it can provide much-needed doses of incentive and encouragement now and then.

If you're a beach person, you'll probably be motivated by oceanside getaways. Ditto if you're a mountain person. If you like rain, go somewhere wet. If you love snow, head north. Draw up your bucket list of natural wonders that you'd like to see in your lifetime, then start making plans. The Northern Lights? The Grand Canyon? The Great Barrier

Reef? Visits to these miraculous sites are often deeply spiritual experiences. Nature's healing majesty awaits.

And don't forget to consider nature adventures. If you're the daring type, you might want to sign up for hot air ballooning, skydiving, whitewater rafting, rock climbing, scuba diving, or snowboarding. What do these have to do with grief, you might rightly ask? The fourth need of mourning is to develop a new self-identity, and if your changing self has always wanted to try one or more of these activities, then now is the time to give them a go. Nature adventures can also help you with the fifth need—search for meaning. People often experience personal epiphanies when they're confronted with moments of encountering danger and overcoming fear.

Finally, "thin places" make wonderful natural destinations. In the Celtic tradition, these are spots where the separation between the physical world and the spiritual world seems most tenuous. They are places where the veil between heaven and earth, between the holy and the everyday, feel so thin that when we are near them, we intuitively sense the timeless, boundless spiritual world. They are often outdoors, in nature, commonly where water and land meet or land and sky come together.

USING CEREMONY IN NATURE

There's something besides nature time that supercharges the healing of grief, and that's ceremony. I believe that combining active mourning in nature with ceremony taps into the most powerful healing energy available.

The word "*ritual*" comes to us from the late-16th-century Latin ritualis and *ritus*, meaning an act performed in a ceremony. That's what grief rituals are—actions that we perform in a certain way and in a certain sequence, for a purpose that has emotional and spiritual meaning and is greater than the sum of its sometimes banal parts.

To incorporate ceremony into your nature visits, simply use intention, actions, symbols, sequence, and spirituality to help yourself fully embrace and integrate your grief.

First, set your intention for the ritual. This will vary depending on what you're struggling with on any given day. For example, you might say to yourself, "In this grief ritual, it's my intention to feel calmer for the rest of this day."

Next, you might stop in several spots on your nature outing and repeat a silent prayer or affirmation.

You might also carry a symbol of your loss in your pocket, perhaps a photo or a small keepsake, and hold that symbol in your hand whenever you are repeating the prayer or affirmation.

Finally, you might close your ritual with an affirmation that restates the intention you set at the beginning of the ritual, such as, "I am ready to return to my day with peace in my heart."

While simple, solitary ceremonies like this are remarkably helpful and can be a mainstay of your engagement with nature, you can also carry out more elaborate ceremonies in nature if you like. For example, for an important anniversary, you could involve others grieving the loss and hold a remembrance ceremony in a meaningful outdoor location.

Indoors, you can also combine ceremony with the elements in the Bringing Nature In section starting on page 43.

I cannot overstate how effective combining nature and ceremony can be in helping you reconcile your grief. I hope you will give it a try.

BRINGING NATURE IN

"Everybody needs beauty as well as bread, places to play in and pray in, where nature may heal and give strength to body and soul."
— John Muir

If you're not the outdoorsy type, or if life demands or mobility issues keep you indoors, you can stay inside and still reap the rewards of nature. And if you're engaging with nature outdoors, bringing nature inside as well will only compound the benefits.

In 1984, environmental psychologist Roger Ulrich studied the medical records of patients recovering from gallbladder surgery at a suburban Pennsylvania hospital. After accounting for all the possible variables, Ulrich and his team discovered that the patient's who'd had bedside windows looking out on leafy trees not only recovered from surgery one day faster, they also needed a lot less pain medication and had fewer postsurgical complications than the patients whose only view was a brick wall.

Wow! Just a view of a tree out a window helped people heal.

Since then, numerous additional studies have documented that merely looking at landscapes—whether from a window, an outdoor vantage point, or even on a computer screen—helps people think better, feel better, and heal faster. We can extrapolate these and other findings in lots of ways in your everyday life.

PLANTS

There are so many ways to bring plant life into your home. Indoors, small potted trees provide that sense of scale and grandeur that actual trees do outside. Smaller potted plants bring in natural colors and textures. Cacti and succulents add lovely variety but are also really easy to care for.

Of course, you can also become an indoor gardener if you want. Viewing plants and having their soothing presence around you is wonderful, but you might also want to try your hand at starting cuttings, growing from seed, shaping and trimming, cultivating herbs indoors, and more. The more you touch and tend, the more in tune with nature you will feel.

And cut flowers bring such life to a room. A simple vase of tulips or dahlias brighten an otherwise plain space, scent the air, and have the power to lift your mood and calm your anxiety.

NATURAL MATERIALS

Another way to bring nature indoors is to integrate natural

and organic materials into the interior of your home. Think small and simple: seagrass baskets, natural wood lamps or end tables, wool throws, beeswax candles, a bowl of shells, rocks you collect on your walks. At the same time, try removing from view any objects that feel cold, artificial, or plastic.

Water is a natural element that can make an interior space feel like you're outdoors. The sound of a small tabletop fountain is soothing, and watching the water spill and drip generates that same calm that watching a river does outside.

Also, natural light makes an astounding difference. Just being exposed to sunlight can lower your risk of heart disease and high blood pressure and help regulate your sleep cycle.

Consider removing window coverings where possible and keeping curtains and shades open as much as you can. Rearrange seating so that you can sit in any sunlight captured through your windows.

NATURE IMAGERY

Remarkably, studies show that viewing nature art yields most of the benefits of spending time in nature. Get a large print of a nature photo or painting that you find soothing or awesome and hang it somewhere you will see it often.

Watching nature videos can have the same effect. Look for TV shows and nature specials that take you into the scenery and places that inspire you most. Try to watch with all of your attention. Notice how you feel after watching one of these shows.

As I've noted, simply looking at nature out your window is also beneficial. Find a good view and a comfortable chair, then allow yourself to do nothing but sit, gaze, and notice. If you'd like, try sketching what you see out your window. Your ability to sketch doesn't matter. The act of moving pen or pencil on paper will help you be mindful and present to the natural view.

ANIMALS

Including companion animals as part of your family is another way to engage with nature indoors (and out). When you think about it, isn't it true that pets bring all of the same benefits to your life that spending time in nature does? That's because they, too, are natural creatures and integral parts of nature.

Many of our companion animals also get us outside, of course. By default, walking a dog, riding a horse, or tending chickens gives us wonderful daily doses of nature time as well as the grief support that our beloved pets are so good at naturally providing us. If you're able to house and care for a companion animal, I highly recommend it.

Nature Heals

NATURAL FOOD

Eating locally grown produce and food made from fresh, local ingredients is a healthy way to bring nature into your life. Look into CSAs (community supported agriculture) in your community. You may be able to have a share of local produce delivered to your door each week. Often you can volunteer at these farms in exchange for the produce, which would be a meaningful way to spend outdoor time.

AROMATHERAPY

Our sense of smell is closely linked with memory. It's also closely linked with nature. When you bring natural smells into your home—via essential oils, scented candles, cut flowers, potted herbs, potpourri, and more—you're immersing yourself in both memory and nature.

Is there a natural scent that you associate with your loss? The piney smell of a Christmas tree, for example, might evoke special holiday memories as well as one of your favorite forest locations. Lighting a pine-scented candle when you are feeling your loss is a way to deepen your engagement with your grief.

Sharing scent-evoked memories with someone else when they arise will also help you meet the sixth need of mourning—reaching out for and accepting the support of others.

NATURE SOUNDS

Did you know that nature sounds alone can calm the body's fight-or-flight response? Listening to them causes your brain to go into wakeful rest, similar to daydreaming. When you can't open your window to birdsong or the rustling of leaves, try listening to nature sounds on apps. For example, the Nature Sounds app is free and includes audio of ocean waves, mountain forests, campfires, and lots more.

Of course, as with certain smells, certain nature sounds may conjure memories associated with your loss. This is also beneficial. Allow yourself to play these memories in your mind, and when you're ready, talk about them with someone who cares about you and will listen without judgment or advice-giving.

Nature Heals

A FINAL WORD

"Climb the mountains and get their good tidings. Nature's peace will flow into you as sunshine flows into trees. The winds will blow their freshness into you and the storms their energy, while cares will drop off like autumn leaves."

— John Muir

I have long referred to grief as a wilderness. I think of it as a vast, mountainous, inhospitable forest. The conditions are brutal, the experience tiring. But the only way to survive this wilderness is to get to know it and to journey through it— for as long as it takes.

Ironically, when you bring your grief wilderness into a real wilderness, things seems to make a little more sense. They fit together, if you will. Natural settings support you in your normal and necessary grief and over time make the whole ordeal a little less brutal, inhospitable, and tiring. Spending time in nature will also feed your spirit and help you find renewed meaning and purpose in your continued life.

I hope you will find ways to integrate nature into your grief journey. The science supports it and, just as important, so does my experience and intuitive understanding. Whenever I take a walk in the desert or hike into the mountains, I will think of you and all the many thousands of grievers I have met in my forty years as a grief counselor and educator. Right now, the trees outside my window draw my eye and soothe my soul. I think I will gaze a while.

THE NATURAL GRIEVER'S BILL OF RIGHTS

"The leaf of every tree brings a message from the unseen world. Look, every falling leaf is a blessing."

— Rumi

1. **I HAVE THE RIGHT TO EXPERIENCE MY OWN UNIQUE GRIEF.**
    I am a unique person with a unique loss experience.
    Spending time in nature helps me understand and accept
    my authentic self.

2. **I HAVE THE RIGHT TO SPEND TIME IN NATURE TO SOOTHE MY PAIN.**
    Nature eases my stress, anxiety, and depression. It brings
    me healthy relief from my pain.

3. **I HAVE THE RIGHT TO SPEND TIME IN NATURE TO ACTIVELY
    ENGAGE WITH MY PAIN.**
    Nature also helps me befriend my pain. When I mourn
    in nature, nature helps support me as I engage with my
    difficult thoughts and feelings.

4. I HAVE THE RIGHT TO EXPLORE MY SPIRITUALITY IN NATURE.

Grief is a spiritual journey, and spending time in nature helps me explore and connect to my spirituality. The combination is powerful.

5. I HAVE THE RIGHT TO BE STILL IN NATURE.

Nature calms me and helps me practice the art of stillness in grief.

6. I HAVE THE RIGHT TO BE ACTIVE IN NATURE.

If I am able, I am free to explore all of the ways I can be physically active in nature. I know that physical activity compounds the healing powers of nature time.

7. I HAVE THE RIGHT TO BE ALONE OR WITH OTHERS IN NATURE AS I ENGAGE WITH MY GRIEF.

Sometimes I may crave solitude in nature, and other times I may crave companionship and the support of fellow human beings. Both are helpful and healing.

8. I HAVE THE RIGHT TO USE CEREMONY IN NATURE.

Adding grief rituals to my nature time supercharges my healing. Using intention, actions, symbols, sequence, and spirituality, I can create and carry out any rituals I want.

9. I HAVE THE RIGHT TO GO OUT INTO NATURE AND TO BRING NATURE IN.

    I go out into nature when and where I can, and I also look for ways to bring nature indoors. Both are part of my healing plan in grief.

10. I HAVE THE RIGHT TO STRENGTHEN MY RELATIONSHIP WITH NATURE TO IMPROVE THE QUALITY OF MY LIFE FOR ALL THE REMAINDER OF MY DAYS.

    Engaging with nature helps me heal my grief. But I am also realizing that spending time in nature is an essential part of my wellbeing no matter what is happening in my life. I will make it a priority to continue spending at least a couple of hours in nature each week for as long as I am able.

The Journey Through Grief
REFLECTIONS ON HEALING | SECOND EDITION

This revised, second edition of *The Journey Through Grief* takes Dr. Wolfelt's popular book of reflections and adds space for guided journaling, asking readers thoughtful questions about their unique mourning needs and providing room to write responses.

ISBN 978-1-879651-11-1 • 152 pages • hardcover • $21.95

First Aid for Broken Hearts

Life is both wonderful and devastating. It graces us with joy, and it breaks our hearts. If your heart is broken, this book is for you. Whether you're struggling with a death, break-up, illness, unwanted life change, or loss of any kind, this book will help you both understand your predicament and figure out what to do about it.

ISBN: 978-1-61722-281-8 • softcover • $9.95

The Wilderness of Grief
A BEAUTIFUL, HARDCOVER GIFT BOOK VERSION OF *UNDERSTANDING YOUR GRIEF*

The Wilderness of Grief is an excerpted version of *Understanding Your Grief*, making it approachable and appropriate for all mourners. This concise book makes an excellent gift for anyone in mourning. On the book's inside front cover is room for writing an inscription to your grieving friend.

ISBN 978-1-879651-52-4 • 112 pages • hardcover • $15.95

All Dr. Wolfelt's publications can be ordered by mail from:
Companion Press, 3735 Broken Bow Road, Fort Collins, CO 80526
(970) 226-6050 • www.centerforloss.com

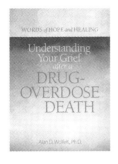

Understanding Your Grief After a Drug-Overdose Death

In this compassionate guide, Dr. Alan Wolfelt shares the most important lessons he has learned from loved ones who've picked up the pieces in the aftermath of a drug overdose. Readers will learn ideas for coping in the early days of their grief, as well as ways to transcend the stigma associated with overdose deaths. The book also explores common thoughts and feelings, the six needs of mourning, self-care essentials, finding hope, and more.

ISBN: 978-1-61722-285-6 • softcover • $9.95

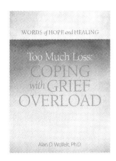

Too Much Loss: Coping with Grief Overload

Grief overload is what you feel when you experience too many significant losses all at once, in a relatively short period of time, or cumulatively. Our minds and hearts have enough trouble coping with a single loss, so when the losses pile up, the grief often seems especially chaotic and defeating. The good news is that through intentional, active mourning, you can and will find your way back to hope and healing. This compassionate guide will show you how.

ISBN: 978-1-61722-287-0 • softcover • $9.95

All Dr. Wolfelt's publications can be ordered by mail from:
Companion Press, 3735 Broken Bow Road, Fort Collins, CO 80526
(970) 226-6050 • www.centerforloss.com

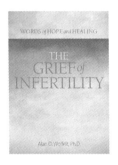

The Grief of Infertility

When you want to have a baby but are struggling with fertility challenges, it's normal to experience a range and mixture of ever-changing feelings. These feelings are a natural and necessary form of grief. Whether you continue to hope to give birth or you've stopped pursuing pregnancy, this compassionate guide will help you affirm and express your feelings about infertility.

By giving authentic attention to your grief, you will be helping yourself cope with your emotions as well as learn how to actively mourn and live fully and joyfully at the same time. This compassionate guide will show you how. Tips for both women and men are included.

ISBN: 978-1-61722-291-7 • softcover • $9.95

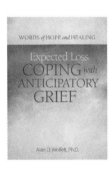

Expected Loss: Coping with Anticipatory Grief

We don't only experience grief after a loss—we often experience it before. If someone we love is seriously ill, or if we're concerned about upcoming hardships of any kind, we naturally begin to grieve right now. This process of anticipatory grief is normal, but it can also be confusing and painful. This compassionate guide will help you understand and befriend your grief as well as find effective ways to express it as you live your daily life.

ISBN: 978-1-61722-295-5 • softcover • $9.95

All Dr. Wolfelt's publications can be ordered by mail from:
Companion Press, 3735 Broken Bow Road, Fort Collins, CO 80526
(970) 226-6050 • www.centerforloss.com

Sympathy and Condolences:
What to Say and Write to Convey Your Support After a Loss

When someone you care about has suffered the death of a loved one or another significant loss, you want to let them know you care. But it can be hard to know what to say to them or to write in a sympathy note. This handy book offers tips for how to talk or write to a grieving person to convey your genuine concern and support. What to say, what not to say, sympathy card etiquette, how to keep in touch, and more are covered in this concise guide written by one of the world's most beloved grief counselors. You'll turn to it again and again, not only after a death but during times of divorce or break-ups, serious illness, loss of a pet, job change or loss, traumatic life events, major life transitions that are both happy and sad, and more.

978-1-61722-305-1 • $9.95 • softcover

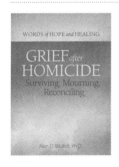

Grief After Homicide:
Surviving, Mourning, Reconciling

Homicide creates a grief like no other. If someone you love died by homicide, your grief is naturally traumatic and complicated. Not only might your grief journey be intertwined with painful criminal justice proceedings, you may also struggle with understandably intense rage, regret, and despair. It's natural for homicide survivors to focus on the particular circumstances of the death as well. Whether your loved one's death was caused by murder or manslaughter, this compassionate guide will help you understand and cope with your difficult grief. It offers suggestions for reconciling yourself to the death on your own terms and finding healing ways for you and your family to mourn. After a homicide death, there is help for those left behind, and there is hope. This book will help see you through.

978-1-61722-303-7 • Softcover • $9.95

All Dr. Wolfelt's publications can be ordered by mail from:
Companion Press, 3735 Broken Bow Road, Fort Collins, CO 80526
(970) 226-6050 • www.centerforloss.com

NOTES:

NOTES:

ABOUT THE AUTHOR

Alan D. Wolfelt, Ph.D., is a respected author and educator on the topics of companioning others and healing in grief. He serves as Director of the Center for Loss and Life Transition and is on the faculty at the University of Colorado Medical

 School's Department of Family Medicine. Dr. Wolfelt has written many bestselling books on healing in grief, including *Understanding Your Grief, Healing Your Grieving Heart*, and *The Mourner's Book of Hope*. Visit www.centerforloss.com to learn more about grief and loss and to order Dr. Wolfelt's books.